Timetable

by Martin Pletsch

© 2010 John Most
ISBN: 978-0-9768938-5-1

Many of these poems originally appeared in *Big Bridge* 17

This book is part of a series of thirteen books.
Each book of poems in the series has been
written by a character invented by John Most.
These characters are entirely fictitious.

AQP Collective
179 Azalea Drive
Afton, VA 22920

AFTER AN IDEA

typologically speaking, awkward giraffes are better
than spoonfuls of honey
however,
faulty truth is not

more prominent than
vulgar simplicity
in pursuit of beauty

HIGH-PRESSURE SYSTEMS

geologically, telling time, as being, is terrifying—for mountains cease
eventually
for doubts'
currents inexplicably
compound people's dim follies

REPLACING THE EAST RIVER

nobody said, "the trains run infrequently after three a.m."
under-the-river
emotions—
her teardrop earrings
swung so carelessly

why

false lighting commands sadness
dull happiness stirs madness

LOVELAND PASS CONTROLS THIS THOUGHT

from fluvial life to flexible stances, outcomes are indeterminable
after certainty
suspicion
after darkness light—guesses
confirmed by quiet yeses

AT NIGHT, KANSAS WILL TELL ANYONE

in what is beyond, a magical promise from temporality that
claims to deliver
a way out
of conditions, work, heartache
via an odd give-and-take

AT MOUNT SINAI HOSPITAL

an apparent apparitional finality
an intangible
ignorance
of life as television
of death as postscripts

A PHONE CALL IMITATES A MOVIE

in the intervening events, a trigger's pulled

the kill shot's
      blurry outcome gawks
at stock-still streets

THE RENTER'S WARDROBE

a free-fall sensation that whispers

we're in love
the city and us—

destitute, it's futile
to think clouds are ignoble

OPPOSING FORCES

compulsions provide temporary relief
from the trembling whole—
putting selves
indivisible
into scenes emendable

STAZIONE DI VENEZIA SANTA LUCIA IN THE EVENING

what do endings mean for the contemporary?
she then he—
timing each other's
commitment
to expression—ready for
facts like closing doors

A LITTLE BRICK HOUSE BEFORE A MOUNTAIN

a primitive position—feet cupped fingers curled
stark dogwood limbs brush
the brick
revealing a trace
  a silhouette to embrace

FLIGHTLESS BIRD, KNOTTED HEART

she is the embodiment of shadow and mist

put her
in ethereal limbo
in the plucked afternoon's glow

BENEATH A PALM TREE IN LA JOLLA

when perceptions are twisted
deletions are rare
but they and nothing can't fade
since all is here then relayed

Timetable was designed and
printed by Red Dot Studio.

www.ingramcontent.com/pod-product-compliance
Lightning Source LLC
Chambersburg PA
CBHW032053290426
44110CB00012B/1072